P9-CLB-616

American Events

THE STOCK MARKET CRASH OF 1929

Nancy Millichap

New Discovery Books
New York

Maxwell Macmillan Canada
Toronto

Maxwell Macmillan International
New York Oxford Singapore Sydney

Book design: Deborah Fillion
Cover photo courtesy of Brown Brothers

Copyright © 1994 by Nancy Millichap

All rights reserved. No part of this book may be reproduced or
transmitted in any form or by any means, electronic or mechanical,
including photocopying, recording, or by any information storage and
retrieval system, without permission in writing from the Publisher.

New Discovery Books
Macmillan Publishing Company
866 Third Avenue
New York, NY 10022

Maxwell Macmillan Canada, Inc.
1200 Eglinton Avenue East
Suite 200
Don Mills, Ontario M3C 3N1

Macmillan Publishing Company is part of the Maxwell Communication
Group of Companies.

First Edition

Printed in the United States of America

10 9 8 7 6 5 4 3 2 1

Library of Congress Cataloging-in-Publication Data

Millichap, Nancy.
    The stock market crash of 1929 / Nancy Millichap. — 1st ed.
        p. cm. — (American Events)
    Includes bibliographical references and index.
    ISBN 0-02-726221-9
    1. Depressions—1929—United States—Juvenile literature. 2. New York Stock
    Exchange—Juvenile literature. 3. United States—Economic conditions—
    1918–1945—Juvenile literature. [1. Depressions—1929. 2. New York Stock
    Exchange—History. 3. United States—Economic conditions—1918–1945.] I.
    Title. II. Series.
    HB3717 1929.D39 1994
    338.5'4'097309043—dc20   93-23310
    Summary: An examination of the events leading up to and following the col-
lapse of the stock market in 1929.

In memory of my mother,

Ruth Turner Millichap

The Bettmann Archive

The front page of the New York Times *the day after Black Tuesday. Oddly, there was little mention of the panic that followed the crash.*

CONTENTS

The Bettmann Archive

Supporters of Prohibition dump barrels of beer into Lake Michigan.

Chapter 1

Out with the Old, In with the New

I t seemed to Nannie Vaughn Turner, a farm wife in Cool Spring, North Carolina, that absolutely everything was changing in 1920. For one thing, young people didn't stay put anymore. Her oldest son, Henry, who was 21, had gone to France to fight in the war. Since he'd been back, he seemed moody and restless. Lately he had been talking about leaving home to get a job in Virginia, rather than work with his father on the farm.

Nannie's 19-year-old daughter, Margaret, was away in Durham, studying to be a nurse. She said that she was going to vote in the next election, now that women had the vote. What was more, she wanted her mother to go with her to the polls. Off at nursing school, Margaret had cut her beautiful, long, blond hair off short—a "bob," she called it. She and all her friends wore dresses so short one could practically see their knees; they reddened their mouths with lipstick and drew black lines around their eyes with greasy pencils. Nannie was shocked. Young ladies hadn't dreamed of wearing makeup or going around half naked when she was a girl.

Nannie's husband, John, wouldn't buy a tractor or a car, but the young man on the next farm rattled by every day in a Model-T Ford that scared the Turners' horses. Her second son, Sam, had come home very excited one November night, claiming that he'd heard the results of the presidential election on something he called a "crystal set" or a "radio." A friend of his in town, who liked to tinker with machinery, had put it together himself. Somehow this contraption let people hear things that were happening in cities hundreds of miles away—even in Washington, D. C. Sam said that Warren G. Harding, the Republican candidate, would win the election. The next afternoon, sure enough, there it was in the paper.

At almost the same time that women got the right to vote, the government had tightened the reins on people who drank alcohol. Nannie herself didn't drink liquor and didn't believe in drinking, so this was one change she approved of. There'd never been any barrooms in Cool Spring, North Carolina, but Nannie understood that even in New York City it was now illegal to sell alcoholic beverages.

There were new temptations, though. A movie theater had just opened in Statesville, the nearest town of any size. Every Saturday night, Henry would hitch up the mules and ride the wagon into town to see the moving pictures. Sometimes he'd take his younger brothers along, and they'd all come home jabbering about the sights of ancient Babylon or the South Seas. It wasn't like the old days, when the only entertainment around might be a traveling play or minstrel show a couple of times a year.

For Nannie Vaughn Turner and for millions of other Americans, 1920 was only the beginning of a decade of dramatic change. Like a powerful windstorm, the Roaring Twenties swept away the old ways of doing things and brought new ways in their place. The changes had begun right after World War I. New technologies—cars, radios, movies—reached into every community in the nation. More young Americans went to high school than ever before, and many more students were going on to college. Americans felt modern and prosperous. They were spending their money to live in new ways, which helped the economy grow quickly.

The old rules did not seem to apply. In what seemed to be a new age and a new world, Americans were full of hope. Many of them thought that the United States would be the first society in the history of the world that would go on improving endlessly. There would be happiness and prosperity for everyone from now on.

The Turners were just one of millions of American families in the 1920s who were still feeling the effects of World War I—the Great War. The war had begun in 1914 and ended in 1918. The Allied forces of Great Britain and France, with many other nations, had fought the Central Powers of Germany and the Austro-Hungarian and Ottoman empires. President Woodrow Wilson had called it "the war to end all wars." In a 1917 speech asking Congress to declare war on Germany, Wilson said that U.S. participation would "make the world safe for democracy."

The United States started sending troops to Europe in 1917, and eventually more than two million Americans joined the fight. "Doughboys," as the American soldiers were nicknamed, arrived in the nick of time. The soldiers of Britain and France were worn out after three years of fighting. Energetic, fresh troops helped win the war. The United States also exported food and weapons to the Allied forces and lent them money to pay for all the things they needed to keep up the fight.

As American soldiers headed for European battlefields, their families and friends back home began taking a personal interest in world events. A popular song of 1918 expressed this interest: "How you gonna keep 'em down on the farm after they've seen Paree?" How would farm boys who had walked down the streets of Paris, France, feel about returning to plowing fields and milking cows?

The war had thrust the United States into the spotlight, making it a major player on the world stage. The war changed Americans' views of the world and of their country.

When World War I ended, delegates from the winning and losing countries worked out the official peace settlement at the French country estate of Versailles. One condition of the peace was that Germany should make payments to the victors called reparations, money to fix the damage the war had done. As a result, Germany faced an even tougher struggle to get back on its feet once the war was over than did other European countries. German towns, bridges, and houses were in ruins. Money that might have been used to build up the country went to pay reparations instead.

The war had shattered all of Europe, not just the losing side. More than 10 million soldiers from the warring nations were dead, the people who had survived were exhausted, and European farmlands, towns, and cities were full of bomb craters.

The United States had come out in far better shape. America had lost fewer of its young soldiers than had France, Germany, and Britain. U.S. territory had not been invaded. And the United States was in good financial condition: It did not have to come up with the money to rebuild houses, roads, and bridges.

Britain and France were not as hopelessly in debt as was Germany, but they did have to repay the loans that they had taken out to wage the war. At the same time, they needed cash to pay for rebuilding. Money was in short supply, imports were expensive, and the American dollar was mighty. The United States was the world's new financial center at the end of the war.

During the war, U.S. manufacturers had been turning out equipment for soldiers. It had been hard for people at home to buy many of the things they wanted. Now exciting new goods and gadgets were pouring out of the factories instead of tanks and guns. Good times were here, and Americans were in the mood to go shopping.

In the 1920s, automobile manufacturing was the fastest growing and most important industry in the country. In 1900 there were only 8,000 cars registered in the entire United States. In 1920 there were more than eight million registered cars, and two million vehicles rolled off the nation's assembly lines that year alone. Nine years later, in 1929, there were more than 23 million registered cars—almost three times as many as at the beginning of the 1920s. Five million cars were made that year. While one American in thirteen owned a car in 1920, the figure had risen to one in six by 1929. Car manufacturers profited from this dramatic increase in production, of course. So did the companies that manufactured the steel, glass, rubber, and other components used in making cars.

At the same time, the construction business had begun booming. With a war on, people had held off on building new houses, stores, and factories. After the war, business picked up. Construction increased every year from 1921 through 1928, so that nearly one and a half times as many new buildings went up in 1928 as in 1921. Many families felt prosperous enough to buy their own houses for the first time instead of continuing to rent. Other families bought more expensive houses than they had owned before.

Enrollment in schools and in institutions of higher learning also increased dramatically, further funding the construction boom. The percentage of young people who went to high school doubled during the 1920s, from 25 percent just after World War I to more than half by 1930. Also, many more of these students were going on to college. About half a million students were in college in 1920. Their numbers doubled to a million by 1929. Schools and universities obviously needed new buildings to make room for all these students.

The popularity of automobiles also helped the construction business. In country areas, dirt roads needed rebuilding. They became paved highways, suitable for automobiles. On the outskirts of cities, entire new suburbs were created. Now that people had cars, they could live farther from the centers of cities and away from railroad and trolley lines. As with the manufacture of automobiles, the growth of construction carried other industries up along with it. The tool and lumber businesses prospered, for example.

Two big changes to the U.S. Constitution followed the world war. In 1919 Congress passed the Eighteenth Amendment, prohibiting the manufacture, sale, and transportation of alcoholic beverages. Congress also passed the Volstead Act, a law that spelled out exactly how Prohibition—the popular name for the consequences of the new amendment—would work.

The push to ban alcohol had come from social reformers and religious leaders. They wanted to keep individuals from destroying themselves and making their families miserable because of alcoholism. However, these reformers ignored actual human behavior. For many Americans, drinking alcohol was an important part of their social life. As a result, liquor remained available throughout the 1920s. What changed were the methods of production, distribution, and sale. Bars and saloons closed down, but popular illegal drinking spots known as speakeasies opened for business, sometimes in the same buildings as the old bars. A new criminal occupation, bootlegging, came into being. Bootleggers took care of the whole business: making, delivering, and selling liquor.

Bootlegging was a vast new area in which organized crime could operate profitably. The president of the American Bar Association, the national lawyers' organization, described the bootlegger as "the spider in the center of the American web of crime."[1] Strictly speaking, buying alcohol from a bootlegger was not illegal. The Eighteenth Amendment did not prohibit buying liquor, but selling it. But an ordinary American was dealing with a lawbreaker any time he or she bought a bottle of wine for a holiday dinner. The world of crime, instead of being shadowy and far away, was right down the street at the speakeasy or the bootlegger's place. It was another area of life in which the old rules that Americans had grown up with did not seem to apply.

Another constitutional amendment passed after World War I had almost an opposite effect on society, loosening it up rather than tightening the reins. In 1920 Congress passed and the states ratified the Nineteenth Amendment, which gave women the right to vote in national elections. The passage of the amendment was to reward women for their service in World War I. It was also a response to more than 30 years of

The Bettmann Archive

A crowded speakeasy does a brisk business.

protests and petitions by suffragists—people who supported women's suffrage, or the right to vote. Not long after they had gained the vote, women themselves began to run for office. Women were elected to the governorships of Wyoming and Texas in 1924.

At the same time, women began to express their freedom in other

The Bettmann Archive

The success of the women's right-to-vote movement and the increasing popularity of the automobile contributed to the free spirit of the Twenties.

ways. Long skirts and corsets went the way of the horse and carriage, along with long hair piled atop the head. Young women wore short, boyish haircuts. Dress hemlines crept upward toward the knee—and then above it. Women everywhere began to wear makeup, and cosmetics soon became a $500-million-a-year industry. Also, some women began to drink and smoke in public. A higher percentage of people than ever before got married, and one marriage in every six now ended in divorce—a record rate.

Americans also had new ways to spend their spare time. Two forms of entertainment captured the country's imagination: movies and radio. While filmmakers had been producing full-length silent movies since 1910, both the number of films being made and the number of theaters soared during the 1920s. By 1926 there were more than 20,000 movie theaters in the country. About 100 million people (of a population of 120 million) went to the movies each week.

In 1927 the movies learned to talk when pictures with sound were introduced. In stylish theaters, uniformed ushers guided families to comfortable plush seats. A world of beautiful people living in faraway places flickered on the screen before them. Advertisements in magazines tempted them: "Out of the cage of everyday existence! If only for an afternoon or an evening—escape!"[2]

Radio was an even newer craze. Several experimental stations started broadcasting in 1919. Soon tens of thousands of Americans were building their own small radio sets to listen in. In 1920 the first commercial station, KDKA in Pittsburgh, went on the air. In 1922 the number of radio stations shot up from four to 576. The sale of radios soared from $1 million in 1920 to $400 million in 1925. Radio gave business a boost in another way: It was a new place to advertise.

All across the country, Americans could listen to the same music and the same dramatic programs. They could also get the news as soon as it happened. News reports broadcast from the places where disasters were happening became very popular.

By 1929 Americans had bought all the cars and houses they could afford. But the factory chimneys kept smoking. New manufacturing methods had made factories more efficient. The same number of workers could make more and more goods. As a result, factories were turning out more brand-new products than people were buying, from cars to sports jackets to porch swings. The president of the National Association of Manufacturers said that 15 to 30 percent more items were being made in 1929 than could be sold. These extra goods piled up in warehouses.

Something similar was happening on U.S. farms, where about one American in three still worked. During the 1920s, farmers bought modern machinery such as tractors and milking machines. These machines made it possible for any one farmer to plant more crops and milk more cows. As a result, farmers were producing more than they could sell, just as manufacturers were.

At the same time, the prices farmers could get for their crops and livestock were falling. During the war, meat, grain, and vegetables from American farms had been exported to Europe. By the early 1920s, however, European farms were again producing their own crops. Prices for American farm products dropped by almost 30 percent in just the four years between 1925 and 1929.

The United States was not the only country with economic problems in 1929. U.S. bankers had been happy to lend money to foreign governments throughout most of the 1920s, and American businesses had been eager to export goods to these countries. Countries that bought or borrowed too much from the United States were now in debt to U.S. banks. By 1929 many foreign countries, especially Germany and nations in Central and South America, owed American banks large amounts of money. These countries could not pay off their loans. The banks that had made the loans lost their money. And American companies, like American farmers, could no longer count on selling their products overseas.

In 1929 the rich were very, very rich. They had a higher percentage of the country's available money than ever before in U.S. history. The richest 5 percent of the people in the country earned a third of the money being made, and the richest 20 percent of the population made more than half of all the money. The wealthiest Americans did not get most of their money

The Bettmann Archive

A typical scene from the Roaring Twenties: A pajama party in the wealthy play-ground of Southampton, New York.

from weekly paychecks. Instead, they received it as interest on their investments or as rent on property they owned. The income-tax rate, having just been introduced to the U.S. in 1906, was much lower than it is today. Low income taxes allowed wealthy people to keep almost all of their earnings. As a result, they kept getting richer.

After the rich had paid for life's necessities—food, shelter, transportation—they had much more money left than did poorer people. With this extra money, they often bought luxuries—furs or jewels, custom-made cars, vacations in other countries—or invested the cash in ways that

The Bettmann Archive

Despite the excesses of the Roaring Twenties, many people in the United States lived in poverty, like this family in a tent city in West Virginia.

would help them get wealthier. What rich people bought, and what they did with their money to make more money, had a big effect on the nation's economy.

The majority of Americans, however, were struggling to make ends meet. A family of four needed an annual income of about $2,000 to pay for basic food, clothing, and shelter. Since the average worker made only $1,280, many households needed two wage earners to make up the difference. In these households, the wife or an older son or daughter worked to boost the income of the "man of the house." Women now made up 25 percent of the workforce. Even with two earners, a working family had little or no money remaining after they had bought groceries and paid the rent. Often there was a shortfall. More than one in five American families had at least some trouble supporting themselves. In January 1929, four million people were out of work. Despite the prosperity of the nation as a whole and of the wealthy few, ordinary citizens benefited only in certain ways. The average paycheck grew little during the 1920s, for example, in spite of all the new products to buy.

When Nannie Vaughn Turner's son Sam listened to the election results of 1920 on his friend's crystal set, the winner was the Republican candidate, Warren G. Harding. He served for only three years, then died suddenly. His vice president, Calvin Coolidge, became president in 1923. Coolidge happened to be at his father's Vermont farmhouse when he heard of Harding's death. It was a new age with new ways, but Coolidge took the presidential oath by the light of a kerosene lamp. In 1924 Coolidge ran for the presidency himself and was elected.

Like Harding, Coolidge accepted the Republican view of America as a society in which making and selling things was the most important activity. Coolidge described it this way: "The business of America is business." He and his administration took a hands-off attitude toward the business community. They devoted themselves to cutting government spending and reducing income-tax rates for businesses and the rich. These cuts and reductions freed the money that sent stock market prices soaring in the 1920s.

Coolidge soon became famous for saying as little as possible—and, when possible, nothing at all. During the summer of 1927, "Silent Cal," as Americans had nicknamed him, announced his decision to give up the presidency. He used the smallest possible number of words: "I do not choose to run in 1928."

To replace Coolidge, the Republicans chose Herbert Hoover as their candidate. An orphan at nine, Hoover had graduated from Stanford

The Bettmann Archive

Herbert Hoover (right) takes the oath of office.

University in California with an engineering degree. He'd run mines in Mexico and China with such success that he was a self-made millionaire ten times over by age 40. A Quaker and a pacifist, Hoover had felt a particular interest in helping unfortunate people when war broke out in Europe. He'd organized war-relief efforts and gotten people in the United States to conserve food at home to help the war effort. Americans had been reading about his successes in the newspapers. They saw him as a man of energy who could get things done.

The Democratic candidate was Al Smith, the governor of New

York. He had been a politician for a long time. As a New York City native, he was at home among all kinds of people. His campaign style was lively, but he had four strikes against him. First of all, he was a city person in a nation that did not yet see itself as urban. Worse, he had come onto the national scene by way of the political organizations of New York City. In the 1920s, everyone had read news stories about the wrongdoings of New York City politicians. Second, he was a Roman Catholic. At that time, no one other than a Protestant had ever been elected to the presidency. Prejudice against Catholics—and against African Americans, Jews, and members of other minority groups—was strong in many parts of the country. Third, Smith favored putting an end to Prohibition. This meant that Protestant church leaders and Southerners who wanted Prohibition to continue came out against him. Fourth, he was a Democrat. Many Americans gave credit for the prosperity of the 1920s to the two previous Republican presidents, Harding and Coolidge. They were not about to spoil things by voting for a member of the opposing party.

In contrast to Smith, Hoover was not comfortable speaking to a rally. He had little of interest or substance to say in his speeches. In fact, he made only seven speeches during his entire campaign. He read them rather than spoke them, scarcely raising his head. Still, when voters looked at his record, they saw a go-getter, a modern expert who could approach and solve problems in a sensible, effective, direct manner. There was a widespread belief in scientific solutions in the 1920s. They were part of the new, improved way of doing things. Who could approach problems more scientifically than the "Great Engineer"?

Herbert Hoover won the 1928 election with 58 percent of the popular vote. In his inaugural address in March 1929, he said: "I have no fears for the future of our country. It is bright with hope." Many of his fellow Americans, living their daily lives in what seemed to be a new world of prosperity and possibility, fully agreed with him.

Chapter 2

Shopping
the Stock Market

D uring the 1920s, one of the biggest changes that took place in American society was in the way people thought about money. Not only did many people have more of it, but they also found that there were new ways in which to make their money grow. Americans heard on street corners and read in newspapers that getting rich was safe and easy. In August 1929, for instance, the respected financier John J. Raskob published an article in the *Ladies' Home Journal* titled "Everybody Ought to Be Rich."

Plenty of people were ready and willing to help Americans try to get rich, because the investment community had also changed. Members of the investment community, once very conservative, now became much more willing to take risks. Their clients, in turn, became freer with their money. Before 1917 most people thought an investment meant keeping money in a bank. Many of these same people now began to turn to other, higher-paying investments.

Americans first learned about other ways to get a return on their money during World War I, when the government offered them a chance to buy bonds to help pay for the war effort. During the war, more than 65 million people bought Liberty Bonds, government bonds that paid a higher rate of interest than did ordinary bank savings accounts. A patriotic American handed over $10 or $25 and received an official-looking certificate, printed with the promise that the government would pay back the money, with interest, at a particular date in the future—perhaps seven years later. Government bonds were one of several kinds of investments called securities. Other securities were stocks and corporate bonds.

Some investors kept buying Liberty Bonds even after the war. Other people tried other types of investments, including the securities of private companies. People who bought a company's bonds were letting that company use their money in return for interest. Essentially the money was a loan for a certain time and rate of interest. Investors in a company's stock actually became part owners of that company. A person with just a few hundred dollars to invest bought shares—small portions of a certain size—in a company. Taken together, all the shares made up the company's stock. Companies held annual meetings of their shareholders (or stockholders), who listened to the managers of the company report on how the business did that year and voted on company decisions. They got one vote for every share of stock they owned.

Stockholders expected to get some return on their money. But unlike people who bought corporate or government bonds, they did not get a promise up front of exactly how much they would make. As part owners, they took a risk that the company would do well and make money for them. One way of making money was the dividend, a percentage of profits that a company might pay to each shareholder. The dividend was set at a rate of so many cents or dollars per share. Shareholders got their dividends once, twice, or four times a year.

Stockholders also made money by waiting until the price of the company's stock went up and then selling their shares. Their profit was the difference between the lower price at which they bought the stock and the higher price at which they sold it. Of course, if a stock's price had dropped between the time an investor bought it and sold it, he or she took a loss rather than making a profit. Some people, known as speculators, bought and sold stocks continuously to take advantage of changes in market prices.

Many of the speculators active in the 1920s were new to the investment game. Unlike more experienced investors, they were not willing to put up with even a small decline in the price of a stock. They expected to make profits quickly, and they would sell at even the slightest price drop. Such jumpiness made stock prices unstable. As a result, some people who bought stock for the long haul lost confidence in the market.

Companies sold two kinds of stock, preferred and common. Investors who owned preferred stock were first in line when dividends were handed out. And sometimes only preferred stockholders got any dividend at all. For example, when General Motors sold fewer cars in 1922 than it had the year before, the company directors decided not to pay any dividend to the holders of the common stock. The preferred stockholders got their dividend, though. The trade-off was that the price of preferred stock went up less, tending to remain in a narrow price range. Of course, if the price of common stock dropped, this stability was a good thing.

Preferred stocks cost more because they guaranteed a return. Before the 1920s, most investors had chosen bonds and preferred stock. If they bought common stock, they took a bigger risk of losing money. But as stock prices rose during the 1920s, common stock became a very popular investment.

Stock markets, the places where people bought and sold securities, existed in major cities across the United States and in other countries, but the New York Stock Exchange was by far the most important one for American investors in the 1920s. This 200-year-old institution did not, itself, offer anything for sale. Instead, it provided a space for trading, the buying and selling of securities. The Stock Exchange's board also made all the rules that governed trading in the United States.

At that time the New York Stock Exchange was a ten-story struc-

The Bettmann Archive

The bustling floor of the New York Stock Exchange.

ture in the style of a Greek temple. Above the entrance, a group of statues represented "Integrity Protecting the Works of Man." The Exchange stood on Wall Street in Lower Manhattan, the southern tip of the island on which the borough of Manhattan is located. Banks and other institutions for handling money surrounded it, and the entire area was known as the financial district. People still refer to the Stock Exchange and the activity that goes on there as "Wall Street." Years earlier, a wall had actually been erected, and later torn down, hence the name Wall Street.

In 1929 at least a million and a half people all across the United States owned securities. Obviously, it would have been impossible for them

The Bettmann Archive

Stockholders watch their fortunes grow as clerks chalk up the latest prices on a large blackboard.

all to come to the Stock Exchange themselves. Instead, they paid fees to professional traders known as brokers to do their trading for them.

Only a limited number of brokers had seats—that is, licenses to buy and sell securities on the floor of the New York Stock Exchange. At the end of the 1920s, membership was limited to 1,375 individuals, all men. As stock prices rose, so did the cost of a seat: from $100,000 in 1922 to a record $625,000 in February 1929.

Nationwide, many more brokers were selling stocks. Brokerage firms in smaller cities and towns across the country telephoned their orders to New York brokerage houses. The New York organizations' members on the Exchange acted for the out-of-town purchasers and sellers. Both the broker who made the transaction directly on the floor and the hometown broker who called in the order received a fee, totaling perhaps 5 percent of the value of the stock they were buying or selling. This fee was added to the investor's cost of trading.

The brokers with seats on the Stock Exchange worked on the trading floor, one of the largest rooms in the world at that time. It measured 140 feet (42 meters) by 115 feet (35 meters), well over half the size of a football field, and had 86-foot-high (26-meter) ceilings. This room contained six trading posts. Clerks who carried out the actual transactions sat at each post, each trading in about 75 stocks. An adjoining annex had opened in 1922 with six more trading posts. The trading floor operated from 9:00 A.M. to 3:00 P.M. Monday through Friday and also half a day on Saturday. Along one side of the room, far above the traders' heads, was a gallery in which visitors might gather to watch the scene.

The stock market—or market, for short—also referred to the general activity of buying and selling stocks. "Playing the market" referred to such activity.

One basic rule of the market was that if someone wanted to sell some stock, someone else had to be available to buy the stock, and vice versa. The demand for the stock determined its price. If a person wanted to sell a very hot stock, any buyer would have to pay a premium price. On the other hand, if the stock was out of favor, the buyer would pay less for that stock. Essentially the stock market was driven by the law of supply and demand: Something in short supply was often very popular and could demand a high price; conversely, something in great supply was worth less because it was easy to obtain, so the price was lower.

Because most stockholders across the nation could not come to the Stock Exchange in person to watch the progress of their stocks, they kept tabs on how a particular stock was doing by consulting the stock ticker. This device received information directly from the Wall Street trading floor by telegraph. It then printed out on a narrow tape of paper, at the rate of 285 characters per second, the current selling prices for stocks. (These strips of paper, tossed from financial district windows, gave the ticker-tape parade its name.) Stock tickers were installed in brokerage houses around the country. During the years of the Big Bull Market—the period of rising stock prices between 1927 and 1929—these brokerage houses were popular gathering places. Stockholders sat around watching their fortunes grow as clerks chalked up the latest prices on a large blackboard.

The speed of the ticker could keep up with the action on normal Wall Street trading days, but on especially active days, when several million shares changed hands, the ticker would fall behind. If the ticker lagged behind the selling action on the floor on a day when prices were *rising*, concern was minimal. People would not find out how much richer they had become until an hour or two after the market was officially closed for the day, but this added to the thrill of speculating.

If the ticker fell behind *falling* prices, it was another matter altogether. On March 29, 1929, for instance, a high rate of stock sales was combined with a sharp fall in prices, and the ticker fell 90 minutes behind the trading on the floor. Investors unable to discover exactly what their stock was bringing in New York panicked and sold at whatever price they could get. Stock prices dropped as much as $17 a share in only five hours.

Brokers outside the Stock Exchange keep track of their stocks by reading ticker tape.

Another way to find out how stocks were doing was to pay attention to stock averages. These statistics gave a general idea of the prices investors were paying for stocks. The best-known stock average was the Dow-Jones, an average price of certain bonds, industrial stocks like U.S. Steel and Standard Oil of New Jersey, and transportation stocks like the Baltimore & Ohio Railroad. Another stock average was the *New York Times* industrial average of 25 "good, sound stocks with regular price changes and generally active markets."[1]

All the averages concentrated on active stocks, the ones that many people were buying and selling. The prices of active stocks went up and down by the largest percentages. Looking at their ups and downs gave brokers and investors an idea of the market's trends.

During the late 1920s, investors wanted more and more common stock, and bankers and brokers were anxious to provide it. One of their methods was to create more investment trusts. These companies made no goods and provided no services. Instead, they existed simply to buy and hold the securities of other companies. This type of business had been almost unknown in the United States before 1920. By 1927, however, there were 160 such trusts, which sold about $400 million worth of investments that year. During 1927, 140 more were formed, and in 1928 another 186 made their appearance. In 1929, 265 were formed. The total assets of investment trusts—the amount of cash or securities they held—was on the order of $8 billion by late 1929.

When the first investment trusts began in the 1880s in Great Britain, the idea was to allow small investors to spread out the risks involved in owning stock. If investors' funds were pooled—were joined, that is, with the other investors' money—each person would be able to own very small amounts, perhaps portions of shares only, in a much larger number of companies than each investor would have been able to purchase alone. The manager of an investment trust used this pooled money to buy stock in dozens of companies.

Some of the stocks that a trust bought might decline in value, but some were likely to increase in value. Investors assumed, of course, that the manager of the trust was an investment professional, a kind of financial wizard, with special skills in making shrewd choices among the available stocks. They also assumed that the stock market was stable and increasing in value.

Investment trusts in the 1920s often were not in fact run by financial wizards, or at least not by wizards interested in making magic for the investors. In addition, many trusts bought securities of companies that produced neither goods nor services. Instead, they bought shares in other investment trusts. In some cases, the other trusts were owned by the same parent organization. National City Bank, for instance, owned several different investment trusts. What gives stock its power to make money is the business it represents. Real profits come from businesses that make and sell goods or services.

Another ingredient in the market of the 1920s was private trading arrangements known as pools. Several investors with a lot of money to spend made deals among themselves to raise or lower the prices of certain stocks. Usually the price of a stock went up when many different investors thought it was worth more than the current price. The investors in a pool knew the stock was really not worth a higher price, but they wanted to make money on it. They did this by getting smaller investors to believe the stock was worth more than the price people were paying for it.

Pools always worked the same way. Investors who wanted to form a pool decided how much they wanted to spend. These amounts might include shares they already held in the particular stock whose price they wanted to push upward. They then hired a manager to act for them. For example, the pool's manager might purchase large blocks of American Tobacco, one popular stock of the 1920s. He might sell some of it and then buy even more the next day. So much trading of one stock got the public's attention. Soon brokers were telling their customers, "Everyone's buying American Tobacco. You'd better pick up a few shares of it so you don't miss out."

At the same time, members of the pool might circulate rumors about the stock. For instance, they might claim that American Tobacco was about to pay a large dividend. To get the word out, they might also pass along false information about the stock to unsuspecting or corrupt news-paper reporters. These reporters would make sure that the flattering rumors about the stock's worth got into the newspapers. Some dishonest journalists received bribes or shares in the pool's profits.

Once the price of the stock had risen as high as the pool manager thought it would go, he gradually began to sell his members' interests. As soon as the pool abandoned a stock, its price fell. The manager and pool members shared the profits of the operation; smaller investors who got out too late took the loss.

For speculators who could afford to organize pools, enormous profits were possible. For instance, the seven Fisher brothers, who had made their fortunes building auto bodies in Detroit, were said to have come east to New York with $300 million available for speculation. They used this money to back pools that bought stock in the Radio Corporation of America and Montgomery Ward, a department-store chain. Their take during a six-week period in late 1928 was between $30 million and $50 million. If the Fisher brothers had put the same money into the bank or invested in bonds paying 8 percent, they would have made less than $2 million.

Not only were such pools legal, they were so much an open secret that the publications of brokerage firms sometimes announced in advance which stocks were to be "taken in hand" by a pool. For investors not belonging to the pool, the trick was to know at what point to get out. Ideally, an investor wanted to sell at exactly the same moment that the pool's manager began to drop its holdings onto the market. In 1929 pool operations manipulated the prices of more than 100 securities.

Such dealings were possible because neither the federal government nor the state of New York put many restrictions on what the New York Stock Exchange did. Instead, the Stock Exchange functioned rather like a private club. It considered the financial interests of its members before anything else, including the public good. The public itself seemed to care little, as long as the market trend was upward and small investors got a share of the profits.

In the 1920s, Americans started buying on credit. Buying on time—that is, on the installment plan—became a popular way to afford major purchases. People who bought their new cars or refrigerators on the installment plan were ready to buy stock the same way. Purchasing stock on credit is called buying on margin. An investor could purchase shares by putting up only a percentage of the price in cash.

Individual brokers had the power to decide how much of the purchase price of a stock the investor had to have in cash. Careful brokers insisted on a sizable deposit, as high as 45 or 50 percent. But not all brokers were careful in the 1920s. In order to get a customer's business and thus make a commission on the sale, many brokers chose to be generous. Some of them let investors buy stock on a margin of as little as 10 percent of the purchase price. That is, the investor would put down in cash only a tenth of what the stock actually cost. His or her broker would then borrow the remaining 90 percent of the money from a bank. Loans that brokers made to allow their customers to buy on margin were called brokers' loans.

For any loan, the borrower had to put down collateral, something of value that the lender kept to make sure that the buyer paid back the loan at a future time. Stocks purchased on margin themselves served as the collateral, or security, for the broker's loan. Until the investor had paid off the loan, the stocks remained at the bank.

If the price of the stock rose, an investor could make remarkable profits putting up little cash. For instance, in January 1929, a broker in Shenandoah, Pennsylvania, offered his customers the chance to buy stock at a 10 percent margin. Maggie Brennan, a high-school teacher, invested only $44 to buy two shares of American Telephone & Telegraph stock, which were worth $440 (10 percent of $440 is $44). Her broker arranged a loan at the Miners' Bank to cover the remaining $396. Brennan never actually saw her stock certificates, which were kept in the vault at the Miners' Bank as security for her loan.

In the summer of 1929, the price of American Telephone & Telegraph stock rose continually. Until Brennan actually sold her stock, though, her profit existed entirely on paper. She stood to lose that profit if prices fell. Just after Labor Day, Brennan sold her two shares for $608. She had made $168 (the difference between $608, what she sold for, and $440, which she bought for, is $168), almost four times her initial investment. After the broker had subtracted his fees and the interest on the money she had borrowed, her profit was $145. She collected the cash just in time to buy an elegant new fall wardrobe.[2]

Things did not work out as well for Thomas Kaunas, a teacher at Shenandoah High School. He chose Chrysler, an automobile-manufacturing company, when he bought stock at a margin of 10 percent in the summer of 1929. He put up $135 to buy 10 shares, worth $1,350, and his broker borrowed the rest from the Miners' Bank.

By early October 1929, the price of Chrysler stock had fallen from $135 to $52 a share. Kaunas's broker called him to ask that he put up more margin—that is, pay more cash. Kaunas still owed the bank more than $1,200, plus interest, and his shares were now worth only $520. He needed to give the broker the difference of $680 in order to keep his investment. Mr. Kaunas certainly did not have an extra $680, an amount equal to almost half his yearly salary. His broker had to sell the Chrysler stock at $52 a share. Mr. Kaunas had lost his original $135 and was heavily in debt to the Miners' Bank. It took him and his family six years to pay off the loan.[3]

Banks charged higher rates of interest on the loans that they made to brokers than on other kinds of loans, such as home mortgages. The rates of interest on brokers' loans changed a lot from day to day. In the summer and early fall of 1929, the interest rate that banks charged speculators ranged from a high of 20 percent to a low of 6 percent. Speculators paid little attention to these rates as long as the prices of stocks were going up. The interest payments were still small in relation to the big profits they were expecting.

Bankers were eager to lend speculators money because they could get high rates of interest. They also thought that brokers' loans were low in risk. If stock market prices started falling, they could demand that the speculators pay off their loans immediately. As a result, the amount of money that banks loaned to speculators kept going up. Eventually, the total of all these brokers' loans topped $8.5 billion.

Some observers realized that if there were a major drop in stock prices, many speculators would not be able to repay their loans. They found the possibility not merely worrisome but frightening. Others, like Edward Henry Harriman Simmons, president of the New York Stock Exchange, claimed that the country had more investment money than it knew what to do with, and the safest place for this money was in the stock market.

In the 1920s, speculators, from small investors like Thomas Kaunas to the big market players like the Van Sweringen brothers of Cleveland, were financing their activity with bank loans. For this reason, banks were in a position to be severely hurt if prices on the stock market fell and did not rise again. Banks did not write their own rules in the way the Stock Exchange did. Instead, most of the banks lending money for speculation were member banks of the Federal Reserve System. If the officials in charge of economic policy grew worried about the possibility of a crash in stock prices, there were actions they could take to control speculation.

The Federal Reserve System was a government organization that made many decisions about the way banks operated in the United States. "The Fed" was created by Congress in 1913 to make sure that the nation's banks could get money to lend out when they needed it. So that the Federal Reserve System would stay independent of politics, Congress set it up in such a way that neither the president nor Congress had direct control over it. The Federal Reserve Board, a group with eight members, ran the Federal Reserve System. One of the president's cabinet members, the secretary of the treasury, served as the chair of this board. Through the secretary, the president had some power to affect the board's decisions about how banks worked.

President Coolidge's secretary of the treasury remained in the cabinet after President Hoover was inaugurated in March 1929. He was the wealthy, powerful industrialist and financier Andrew Mellon. Secretary Mellon had proved to be a very good friend indeed to his Wall Street colleagues throughout his years on the cabinet. He had taken many actions to benefit them, such as cutting taxes.

Twelve Federal Reserve Banks around the nation carried out the decisions that the Federal Reserve Board made about banking. These Federal Reserve Banks provided services to individual member banks in their districts. In 1929 about 9,000 member banks belonged to the system. Member banks could turn to their district Federal Reserve Bank if they needed credit.

For instance, a small-town California bank had decided to lend a grocer money to build a new store. However, several other businessmen in town had just borrowed money for a new office building. All the money that the bank had available was out on loan. By borrowing the money from the Federal Reserve Bank of San Francisco at 4 percent interest, the bank could still make the loan. It lent the grocer the money it got from the Federal Reserve Bank, charging him 5 percent interest.

Of the 12 district banks, the Federal Reserve Bank of New York was the most powerful in the 1920s. Then, as today, New York City was the largest city in the country and the nation's financial hub as well.

The Federal Reserve Board could control stock speculation by changing the rate of interest their member banks could charge. If the rate fell, taking out loans became cheaper and more popular; but if the rate rose, borrowing money became more expensive. Lower rates to banks made more money available to speculators and encouraged stock purchases, while higher interest rates made it less attractive for speculators to take out loans.

The Federal Reserve's interest rate was a reasonable 4 percent or 5 percent in the 1920s. These low interest rates made buying stock on margin more attractive. They helped to create the Big Bull Market of 1927 to 1929.

Chapter 3

The Big Bull Market

Everyone seemed to be rushing into the market in the 1920s, from wealthy older men to young women speculating with their grocery money. In the spirit of the times, the popular magazine *The Saturday Evening Post* printed this verse:

> Oh, hush thee, my babe, granny's bought some more shares,
> Daddy's gone out to play with the bulls and the bears,
> Mother's buying on tips, and she simply can't lose,
> And baby shall have some expensive new shoes![1]

Daddy's "bulls and the bears" referred to Wall Street's nicknames for speculators with different ideas about what would happen to stock prices. Bears were speculators who invested money in the expectation that prices would go down; times when stock prices were falling were called bear markets. Bulls expected that prices would be going up and invested with that belief in mind; a bull market was a time of rising prices.

Both bulls and bears managed to make money in the early 1920s. William Durant, the founder of General Motors, bought and sold so many rising stocks during the decade that the financial newspapers referred to him as "The King of the Bulls." Another big trader, Jesse Livermore, made his fortune by speculating in bear markets. He did well enough during a slump in the market in 1921 to buy himself not one but several mansions around New York City.

More traders began to speculate in common stock as the decade continued. Speculation was responsible for the surge in price of the Radio Corporation of America stock, for instance. "Radio," as everyone called it, was one of the biggest success stories on Wall Street. Its price per share rose from $2.50 in 1921 to $85 in 1927, even though it never paid a dividend.

After 1927, more and more ordinary Americans joined the rush to make money by buying and selling common stock. Before this, small-town investors like Maggie Brennan had believed that smart investors bought only preferred stocks and bonds. But such investments paid back no more than 6 percent or 8 percent a year, compared with an average return of 16.5 percent a year on common stocks between 1922 and 1929.

The term "Big Bull Market" refers to the long period from about 1927 to late 1929 during which stock prices moved up dramatically, encouraging wild speculation. It was not surprising that many people headed for the local brokerage office. With the prices of common stocks soaring upward, they asked themselves, Why settle for less than a killing? Otto Kahn, an important investment banker, noticed the trend and said with satisfaction, "Democracy has found its way into finance. We have begun to become a nation of investors."[2]

Even during the Big Bull Market, however, no more than three million Americans—one in 40—owned stock. Many of them were newcomers to stock trading, and these newcomers tended to be bulls, optimists who believed that the market would continue up and up. In fact, many new speculators had never experienced a serious fall in stock prices. The mood

Wall Street teems with brokers and investors during the height of the prosperous Bull Market.

on Wall Street, and the news in the papers, encouraged them to believe that the boom could go on forever. An editorial in the *New York World* declared: "Nothing matters as long as stocks keep going up. The market is now its own law."[3]

The size of the Big Bull Market was partly a matter of the amount of stock being bought and sold. A day on which two million shares changed hands on the New York Stock Exchange had been big news early in the 1920s. The first day on which four million shares were bought and sold was in 1928, and the first five-million-share day came later that same year. In November 1928, just after the presidential election, there was a whole week during which so many stocks changed hands that the stock ticker did not finish recording the day's trading until two hours after the market had closed.

The Big Bull Market was also big in terms of price increases. The stock averages rose sharply, and that encouraged more speculation. In 1927 stock prices rose by 20 percent and stock sales by 24 percent. The *New York Times* industrial average rose by 26 percent in 1928. And by the end of the Big Bull Market in 1929, the price of an average share of common stock had risen to $225, almost twice its 1927 level of $115.

Prices climbed steeply for stock in companies making the most popular new products, like the Radio Corporation of America and General Motors. In the year 1928 alone, the price of Radio increased almost fivefold, from $85 to $420 a share. Speculators also paid more and more for stock in appliance companies like Westinghouse, department-store chains like Sears, Roebuck and Montgomery Ward, chains of movie theaters, aviation companies, and companies that made the steel that went into cars. The new investment trusts were also very popular. About 200 stocks were referred to as the "speculative favorites," the ones everyone wanted to buy.

Speculators found ways and means to trade no matter where they were. Broadway performers, including Groucho and Harpo Marx, rushed to backstage telephones between acts to call their brokers. Ocean liners sailing to and from Europe had brokerage branch offices with shortwave radios and ship-to-shore telephones for customers. At a national golf championship in California, one brokerage firm set up a temporary office in a tent near the 18th hole.

Early in 1929, the Federal Reserve Board found itself in a fix. The question its eight members faced was whether to raise the interest rate they charged to their member banks. As the board members saw it, having so much money out on loan to stock speculators damaged the country's long-term prospects. Not enough money was left for real business activity, such as building new stores and factories. And yet if the board raised the Fed's interest rates sharply to cut the amount of money available for speculation, stock market prices would almost certainly plunge. They might carry the whole economy down along with them.

Andrew Mellon, secretary of the treasury and chair of the Federal Reserve Board, was against raising interest rates. Following his lead, the board decided to sound a warning rather than make any bold move. In February 1929, they sent a letter to the 12 Fed Banks urging them in strong terms not to lend Federal Reserve money for speculation but instead to back real business investment with their loans. Member banks were still free to lend speculators money that they had not borrowed from the Federal Reserve Banks.

Even if the Fed controlled all the money in its member banks, it might not have slowed speculation by much. Banks were only one of the resources available to the determined speculator. Attracted by the high interest rates being charged for brokers' loans, many corporations were eager to lend speculators money. Some corporations found that they could make more money lending funds to stock speculators than by actually producing and marketing goods and services.

If you were to read a 1929 newspaper today, you might think that everyone in the country was a stockholder. In fact, Wall Street's ups and downs were far removed from the daily lives of most Americans. Many of the three million stockholders in the United States owned just a share or two, and many of them had paid cash. Fewer than half a million people had margin accounts with brokers. Stock speculators represented less than half of 1 percent of the population of the United States.

The surprising thing about the Big Bull Market, then, was not that everyone was involved. Rather, it was the amount of attention paid to the market and the people who were participating in it. A British writer who came to New York in 1928 put it this way: "You could talk about Prohibition, or Hemingway [the famous author], or air-conditioning, or music, or horses, but in the end you had to talk about the stock market, and that was when the conversation became serious."[4] The talk on the street, in offices, and at dinner parties was full of the doings of the market, and so were the news media.

The newspapers began printing more and more financial news in the 1920s. Stock market news moved from the paper's back section to its front page. In the spring of 1929, financial stories took up a third of the news space in the *New York Times.* Small publishers brought out stock market tip sheets that sold for a dime. These sheets spelled out Wall Street activity in ways that new speculators could understand.

In addition to the financial reports, the papers covered human-interest stories of those who had made fortunes. A nurse made $30,000 by buying on the advice of her grateful patients. A rancher in Wyoming did well, even though he lived 30 miles (48 kilometers) from the nearest town, trading a thousand shares a day by telephone. An Illinois telegraph operator who sent the orders of wealthy local men to their brokers bought the same stocks they did and became wealthy himself.[5]

Big speculators, the ones who controlled pool operations and made fortunes in a few weeks, became well-known personalities. Anything they had to say was newsworthy. Reporters scanned the passenger lists of ships returning from Europe for their names and hurried down to the docks to interview them and snap their pictures. The nickname for these large-scale speculators was "plungers." Ordinary people admired these dashing risk-takers, who seemed to fling their money into the market as though they were diving into a deep pool of water.

Many of the plungers were men who had made fortunes in the automobile or other manufacturing industries in what was then called the West—the area south of the Great Lakes that we know today as the Midwest. The most famous of these Midwesterners was William Durant. Jesse Livermore, who rode around New York in a yellow Rolls-Royce, was among the flashiest. Arthur Cutten had already made $10 million on the Chicago Stock Exchange when he started participating in pools in the New York market. Smaller speculators kept a close eye on these men, especially on what they were buying and selling. Just the knowledge that Cutten, for instance, was buying a particular stock helped push that stock's price higher.

Before 1929, the summers of the 1920s were slow times at the Stock Exchange. Brokers and speculators headed off on vacation to Bar Harbor, Maine, where the Rockefellers were just one of the wealthy families with an estate, or to the vast fancy lodges of the Adirondack Mountains in upstate New York, or to Europe if they had had an especially good year at the market. The summer of 1929 was a different matter, though. Trading was so brisk that many traders stayed in town.

More than 95 million shares were traded in August, making the month one of the busiest trading months in Wall Street history. Prices were 30 percent higher than they had been in August 1928, and they were still going up. Stocks gained almost $5 billion in value just in the month of August.

Much of the money being used to buy all these stocks was borrowed. Brokers' loans increased by $400 million in June, another $400 million in July, and more than $400 million in August. By the end of August, speculators owed banks more than $7 billion for the stock they had bought on margin.

The Bettmann Archive

*Convinced that the good times would last forever, happy investors watch the value
of their stocks increase steadily.*

At the same time, these brokers' loans were getting more expensive. The rate charged for borrowing to speculate had ranged between 6 percent and 15 percent during the summer months. In August the Federal Reserve Board finally raised its interest rate. This change caused a sharp decline in stock prices. Yet the market recovered quickly, and prices started up toward new heights again. To borrow at 6 percent, or 10 percent, or even 15 percent in order to buy a stock that could not possibly be expected to pay dividends as high as 5 percent made sense only for speculation, not for long-term investment. Some observers felt that speculators were behaving like gamblers at a roulette table.

Tuesday, September 3, 1929, was the day after Labor Day. As in every other year, this day was considered the beginning of a new season, the day to return to "serious business" after the summer's lull. On that day, prices soared upward yet again. With almost 4.5 million shares traded, the *New York Times* industrial average reached $452. No one realized it at the time, but the prices of many of the leading stocks that day were at the highest level they would reach during the next quarter of a century. The Big Bull Market had reached its peak.

Chapter 4

The Crash

O nce Labor Day, 1929, had come and gone, some brokers noticed a disturbing trend. Many of their wealthiest clients were selling large amounts of high-quality stock. These customers had been investing in securities long before the Big Bull Market had gotten under-way. Now, instead of buying other stock with their profits, they seemed to be leaving the market entirely.

The biggest speculator of them all, William Durant, was reported to be selling much more stock than he bought. According to records that became public only years later, in 1929 the "King of the Bulls" sold stock worth more than $244 million and bought stock worth just $204. Joseph Kennedy, the father of future President John F. Kennedy and a shrewd speculator, sold all his stocks except those in the film industry. He told a surprised friend, "Only a fool holds out for the top dollar."[1] The respected financier Bernard Baruch also sold his stock holdings and privately urged his friends to sell theirs. To avoid any chance of starting a panic, though, he said publicly that stock prices would probably continue to rise.

Seeing plungers like Durant and experienced investors like Kennedy and Baruch selling out made bankers and brokers uneasy. They did not want the market to run out of people who wanted to buy and who expected a rapid increase in price. If it did, borrowing money to buy stock—that is, buying on margin—would become pointless. Everyone would want to get out, and they would all try to sell at the same time. The boom would end, and not quietly. Instead, the bottom would drop out.

Roger Babson was a Massachusetts economist who had been predicting a disaster in the market for more than two years. On the Thursday after Labor Day, he made a speech to the National Business Conference. Once again, he told his audience that desperate times were ahead. "Sooner or later a crash is coming," he said, "and it may be terrific. . . . There may be a stampede for selling which will exceed anything that the Stock Exchange has ever witnessed."[2]

Earlier, most people had ignored Roger Babson's remarks. But on September 5, 1929, both stock prices and the amount of money out on loan to speculators stood at an all-time high. Brokers on the New York Stock Exchange and their customers throughout the country were nervous about this. When Babson's speech came over the ticker tape in the middle of that afternoon, many felt the urge to sell. More than two million shares changed hands in just the last hour of trading, and prices fell sharply.

Over the next two days prices recovered, but they fell again in mid-September and continued to slide gradually downward. Some of the stocks that had seen the most rapid increases in price during the Big Bull Market, such as U.S. Steel and Radio, were now dropping by a few dollars every day. Trading volume was high, with at least four million shares being sold on most days. And people were still speculating. The volume of brokers' loans—the money extended on credit to buy stocks—rose by almost $670 million that September, the largest increase to date in a single month.

Investors were nervous. Also, some of them were worried by the economic news. The declines were slight, but steel production, automobile sales, and construction were all headed in the same direction as stock prices: down. Events in Europe were another source of concern, because some American businesses counted on international trade. Germany had been depending on American loans to pay its reparations, the money it owed to countries that it had fought against in World War I. Now these loans had run out, and Germany had to rely on its own resources and its own economy.

Many ordinary Germans were out of work. German farmers were so poor that they could not buy fertilizer to help their crops grow. Playing on the discontent of the German people, Adolf Hitler and his National Socialist (abbreviated to NAZI) party were becoming more powerful.

In Britain, meanwhile, the farmers were suffering the effects of low prices. Young people were leaving the countryside to look for city jobs. But these were not so easy to find. Many working men and women had been unable to get jobs for years, especially in the coal-mining areas. In some cases, they and their families were selling furniture to buy food. By 1929, the unemployment rate was 70 percent in some northern areas of England.

The investment scene in Britain was similar to that in the United States, with a booming market and many speculators. British investors, like their American counterparts, had been active in the Big Bull Market, pouring their money into American stocks. On September 20, the London papers reported that Clarence Hatry's financial empire had suddenly collapsed. Hatry had built up his fortune in dishonest ways, including various kinds of stock fraud. British investors worried about the safety of their money, and prices declined sharply on the London Stock Exchange. At the same time, the Bank of England raised its interest rate, making it more expensive to borrow money and more difficult for British speculators to trade on the New York Stock Exchange.

By the middle of October, the mood of optimism with which the fall season had begun had changed to one of alarm. Investors and brokers alike were fearful. As prices declined, stocks purchased on margin could no longer hold their value as collateral for the loans that investors had taken out to pay for them. Brokers phoned investors and asked them for more margin—that is, for more cash to hold the loan.

Take, for example, the two shares of American Telephone & Telegraph stock that Maggie Brennan sold on September 3, 1929, for $608. George Bailey, a Chicago post-office employee, bought two American Telephone & Telegraph shares on margin that same day. Bailey's broker was offering a margin of 20 percent, so Bailey paid only $124 in cash toward the purchase price. To get the remaining $484, Bailey's broker arranged a bank loan. But in October, the value of Bailey's two shares dropped to $404. They were no longer worth as much as he had borrowed to buy them.

Bailey's broker called him and told him that he would have to put up more margin in order to keep his loan and his stock—that is, pay the bank the $80 difference between what his stock was now worth and what he owed the bank for it. Meanwhile, the price of the stock kept dropping. If Bailey did manage to come up with the extra money, he would soon get another call asking for yet more margin. He faced losing his investment and still being in debt to the bank.[3]

Bailey—and many people who had bought their stocks on margin—had really not foreseen the possibility of a decline. Many of them had no additional money to invest. Not surprisingly, these investors were desperate to sell before prices dropped further and left them hopelessly in debt. More people wanted to sell, and there were fewer eager new buyers. As a result, prices kept falling. The downward trend seemed as unstoppable as the upward trend.

Wall Street speculators reassured one another in several other ways as stock prices declined. The economic position of the country was sound. The Federal Reserve Board had sensible policies about credit: It had not raised the interest rate since August, for example. And they were counting on help from large-scale investors if things got much worse.

Nervous brokers, desperate investors, and financial writers all believed that the large-scale players of the Big Bull Market could not afford to let stock prices fall. They had too much to lose. Midwestern plungers like Durant, the investment trusts, and bank officials would form a pool. This pool would provide organized support, buying up large amounts of stock. That way, stock prices in general would not drop below their present levels, and investors would not lose their money. Or so rumor had it.

After taking their worst plunge of the year on October 3, prices recovered on October 5. The *Wall Street Journal* noted triumphantly that "the market has been able to score a quick comeback."[4] Moderate rises continued for almost two weeks. Then on October 16, a committee of the Investment Bankers Association reported to its convention that speculation was at a dangerous level. Stocks were selling for prices far above what they were worth, the committee said. At least partly in reaction to this report, prices on Wall Street fell sharply again. Although they bounced back the next day, the trend all that week was downward. Still, some well-known experts continued to express confidence in the market. On October 15, Yale economist Irving Fisher made a public statement that would soon haunt him. "Stock prices have reached what looks like a permanently high plateau,"[5] he said.

Monday, October 21, proved to be a model of how things would go during the next few weeks. Many more stocks than usual were up for sale, with more than six million shares changing hands. In addition, the volume of sales was very high. As a result, the reports coming over the stock ticker, which supposedly represented up-to-the-minute prices, fell behind the action on the floor by the time the exchange had been open for only ten minutes.

The ticker had been slow on days of rising prices during the summer. Since the price decline on March 26 when the ticker had dragged behind the action, it had not lagged on a day of falling prices. This time, the ticker continued to lag ever farther behind as the day went on. The ticker recorded the day's last transaction at 4:40, an hour and 40 minutes after the exchange had closed.

For almost the entire day, then, panicky stockholders in New York and in brokerage offices across the country had no way of telling exactly how their individual stocks were doing. With prices falling generally, investors naturally assumed the worst about what was happening to the prices of the stocks they owned. Fear led them to give their brokers sell orders. Repeated hundreds of times, this release of more stocks for sale increased market volume and led to additional price declines. Prices of the most popular stocks fell only a few dollars that day, since optimistic bargain-hunters were still buying them.

There was a slight recovery on October 22, with prices rising from $1 to $16 a share on average. The optimistic Professor Fisher spoke out again, declaring that stock prices were still a bargain. He played down the previous day's losses, calling the decline "a shaking out of the lunatic fringe that attempts to speculate on margin."[6] The *Wall Street Journal* called the price drop "a very bad break, the most severe in a number of years,"[7] but the paper also hinted that great bargains were now available. At the same time, Roger Babson was sticking to his predictions of disaster. He urged people to sell their stocks and invest in something with a more stable value: gold.

On October 23, too, sales were strong and prices held firm until noon. Then the volume of selling increased and prices began dropping. A total of $4 billion in stock values was lost that day, nearly 5 percent of the total value of all the stocks bought and sold on the New York Stock Exchange. If prices continued to fall like this each day, stocks would be worth nothing at all in less than a month. The popular, active stocks of the *New York Times* industrial average dropped from $415 to $384 per share. All the gains these important stocks had made since the previous June evaporated in a single afternoon.

In the wild scramble to sell, brokers raced to the telephones along the edges of the Exchange trading floor. Many investors who might not otherwise have sold that day heard the demand for "more margin." If they could not raise the additional cash, their brokers sold them out—which meant more stock on the market. During the boom, speculators seemed to have forgotten the laws of supply and demand. A stock was worth only what someone would pay them for it. In order to sell, they needed buyers. Now those who wanted to sell greatly out-

The Bettmann Archive

Searching for news of their investments, worried speculators crowd the streets of the financial district.

numbered those who wanted to buy, with the result that prices kept drop-ping until they got low enough that someone would pick up the stock as a bargain.

The rush of trading was like the high-volume buying and selling in a department store during a going-out-of-business sale, though the mood was very different. In just the last hour of the business day, over two and a half million shares changed hands—more than were sometimes traded in an entire day. The ticker again dropped far behind the action on the floor. From coast to coast, investors were tormented by uncertainty about their losses. An ice storm in the Midwest disrupted communications, further preventing investors in that part of the country from getting accu-rate information.

All the earlier price declines in the fall of 1929 had been referred to in the press as "breaks." For the first time, the events on Wall Street on October 23 were widely described as a "crash." Not surprisingly, investors all across the country telephoned their brokers with sell orders when they read or heard the alarming news of Wednesday's trading.

All those sell orders were clutched in brokers' hands when the starting bell opened trading the next day, October 24. In the desperate frenzy of selling, prices plunged downward by $5, $10, or even $15 a minute. There were unbelievable moments when some stocks found no buyers at all, no matter how low the price went.

For their own financial protection, many out-of-town brokers had placed stop-loss orders with their agents on the Exchange floor. These were instructions to sell the stocks of investors who had not responded to their brokers' calls for more margin if the prices of those stocks dropped below a particular level. As prices fell, the stop-loss orders were carried out. Blocks of stock came up for sale automatically, adding to the volume and speeding up the drops in prices. And as prices fell, they triggered still more stop-loss orders.

Huge blocks of stock—lots of 6,000, 10,000, 20,000, or more shares—

were dumped onto the market. Blocks of this size represented very large sums of money. A 10,000-share block of a $200-a-share stock, for instance, was worth $2 million—or only $1.5 million if the price dropped to $150 a share. In all, nearly 13 million shares changed hands that day, almost three times as many as on even a heavy trading day in the summer or earlier in the fall.

Such an unusually high number of sales meant that once again the ticker lagged behind the action on the floor. With ticker prices off by as much as $30 a share, out-of-town brokers and investors who were trying to decide whether to sell could not get an accurate idea of current prices. By the closing gong on what came to be known as Black Thursday, the ticker was more than four hours behind.

People gathered in the street outside the Exchange as the day wore on and the news got worse. The police commissioner of New York City sent more than 500 detectives, foot patrolmen, and mounted police into the Wall Street area to keep the peace. A workman was making repairs on a roof near the Exchange, and rumor spread through the crowd that he was a disappointed investor about to jump to his death. Possibly this rumor was the start of all the stories told during the following days of speculators committing suicide by leaping out of the windows in the financial district.

The crowds outside the Exchange could hear a weird roar. A thousand brokers were crowding the floor of the Exchange that day, all shouting out prices. More than 700 people had gathered in the visitors' gallery overlooking the trading floor, and the stockholders among them were screaming in horror as their fortunes disappeared right before their eyes. The noise was deafening. At 12:30 P.M., Stock Exchange officials showed the visitors out and closed the gallery.

By then, though, the worst of the day's panic was nearly over. In a meeting at the offices of the widely respected investment banking house of J. P. Morgan and Company, five of the nation's most important bankers

The Bettmann Archive

The scene outside the New York Stock Exchange after the crash hit.

at last agreed to provide some of the long-expected organized support. Together, they would put up $340 million, more money than any pool had yet directed at the market. The bankers wanted first of all to protect their own direct interests, but they also hoped to restore investors' confidence in the market. They wanted their pool to get the maximum possible publicity.

After the meeting, Morgan's senior partner, Thomas Lamont, met with the press. He made a classic understatement: "There has been a little distress selling on the Stock Exchange."[8] Less than an hour later, Richard Whitney, the vice president of the New York Stock Exchange and the broker who represented J. P. Morgan and Company at the Exchange, went onto the floor. Everyone watched as he headed for the post where steel stocks were traded. There he loudly and confidently agreed to buy a large block of U.S. Steel shares at the prevailing price. The brokers cheered. They saw Whitney's purchase as a demonstration that the bankers were not going to let prices keep falling. Whitney moved on from post to post, using money from the bankers' pool to buy millions of dollars' worth of stock at the current asking prices.

Whitney's purchases had just the effect that the bankers had hoped for. Word spread quickly that the market was receiving organized support, and prices began to go back upward. No more stop-loss orders were triggered. Some of the value that had been lost that morning was recovered in the hours after the bankers provided support. In fact, the drop in the *New York Times* average for the day as a whole was less than a third of its drop on Wednesday. But many investors had sold, or been sold out by their brokers for lack of margin, during the panicky hours of the morning. John Hersch, a young Chicago businessman, had been buying on margin. He saw his entire savings of $3,000 dwindle to $62 that Thursday, known as Black Thursday. To him and to thousands of other investors around the country, this late-day recovery was an additional insult rather than a comfort.

That Friday, and during the half-day session that was held on Saturday in the 1920s, the volume of buying and selling was high. Prices remained steady. Bankers who had bought stocks to give the market support were able to sell them, either at a profit or without a loss.

Over these two days, the press was full of expressions of optimism and confidence from bankers, brokerage houses, economists, and politicians alike. The leading brokerage houses sent telegrams to their clients predicting that prices would make a quick recovery. Even President Hoover, pressed by the powerful bankers to make an encouraging public statement, proclaimed that "the fundamental business of the country—that is, the production and distribution of commodities—is on a sound and prosperous basis."[9] The bankers had wanted him to go further—to say, for instance, that stocks were now a bargain. But for years President Hoover had been worried about the level of speculation. He refused.

If most people believed what they read in the papers and heard on the radio, they surely did believe that the worst was over. Stocks were now cheap, reported the financial news writers, and buyers would be rushing to purchase them. Brokerage houses placed ads in the weekend papers encouraging new investment. One read, "We believe that the investor who purchases securities at this time…may do so with utmost confidence."[10]

Over the same weekend, sell orders from country bankers and mistrustful investors had piled up. Monday, October 28, was another terrible day. Nine million shares changed hands, and price declines for the day were much worse than they had been on Black Thursday. The *New York Times* industrial average was down by $49 for the day, a worse decline than the entire previous week. Between $10 billion and $14 billion in stock values was lost, more than all the money then in circulation in the country. And the ticker once again ran late.

Late that afternoon, the big bankers met again at Morgan's. They still had money remaining in their $340 million pool. But they decided that they would offer no more organized support, now that they had managed

The Bettmann Archive

A newspaper headline sums up the crash.

to shore up prices enough to get out themselves. After meeting for two hours, they gave the press a statement spelling out just what they did—and did not—intend to do. They would not try to maintain any particular level of prices or protect profits. What they did intend was to assure an orderly market in which there would be a buyer—at *some* price—for every seller.

For the desperate investors of America, this was not encouraging news. Many of them were ruined. An insurance representative watching the ticker in Kansas City suddenly shouted, "Tell the boys I can't pay them what I owe them!" and shot himself.[11] Comedian Groucho Marx, who had been buying Auburn Auto stock on margin, lost his entire investment of a quarter million dollars and was heavily in debt. But there were also those who took a happy-go-lucky attitude. A young widow who had lost most of a $1 million nest egg remarked, "I had a perfectly stunning time while it lasted. I never before knew what fun it was to make money."[12]

October 29, Black Tuesday, was the single worst day of the crash and, to many people, the worst day in the history of the New York Stock Exchange. The volume of transactions was even greater than it had been on Black Thursday. Now it was the big speculators who were desperately dumping stock onto the market, sometimes in blocks of up to 50,000 shares. Nearly $16\frac{1}{2}$ million shares were sold, a record volume that was to stand until 1968. So many sell orders accumulated in brokers' offices that the clerks who telephoned them to the Exchange floor fell two hours behind. And the losses were almost as bad as they had been the day before. The *Times* industrial average declined another $43, while the Dow-Jones industrials fell $48. Overall, prices had tumbled back to the levels they had been an entire year earlier. Prices rose shortly before the market closed for the day, or the losses would have been even worse.

The investment trusts that had been organized to trade one another's stock suffered some of the worst losses of Black Tuesday. To take two of the most popular, the price of a share of Goldman Sachs Trading

Corporation lost almost half its value in that single day, falling from $60 to $35, and Blue Ridge dropped from $10 to $3, losing two-thirds of its value. An investor who owned 100 shares of Blue Ridge saw their value fall from $1,000 to $300 in a mere five hours.

The stock of some trusts went begging, with no takers at any price. The era of trusts, organizations that invested not in productive companies but in other trusts, was over. Now that public confidence in the market had dried up, they were doomed.

As on the earlier days of the crash, lights burned late on Wall Street as brokerage houses tried desperately to catch up on their paperwork. Across the country, large and small investors alike covered their scratch pads with depressing calculations. People who had speculated on margin and those who had gotten into the market most recently and paid the highest prices suffered most, but virtually everyone in the market lost a significant portion of their investment.

Large and small investors alike saw that the crash had taken not merely their paper profits but also their hopes and, in many cases, all their savings. The Fisher brothers lost $200 million of their $300 million fortune. The boxer Jack Dempsey, once a millionaire, was broke. Comedian Eddie Cantor had $60 left and was $285,000 in debt for his brokers' loans. The Big Bull Market was dead and buried, and the sense of well-being and prosperity that so many Americans had enjoyed throughout the previous decade was buried with it.

Chapter 5

Sliding Down
Prosperity Hill

I n official circles, Black Tuesday seemed to spell the end of the Big Bull Market. To many others, it slammed the door on a decade of free and easy living and spending. On Wednesday, however, some individuals were already feeling optimistic again. Perhaps they had been hasty in their evaluation of the preceding week.

Stock prices rose, and some investment trusts and a few professional speculators who had gotten out before the worst days of the crash were buying at what looked like bargain prices. Even the distinguished financier Bernard Baruch bought a large block of American Smelting stock. Could a recovery be underway already?

Over the weekend, however, sell orders piled up, and on the following Monday prices nose-dived once again. They kept dropping for another two weeks, reaching their lowest level of 1929 on November 13. That day the average price of the *Times* industrial stocks was $224, down from $452 after Labor Day. In a little over two months, the market had lost 50 percent of its value. The total loss was at least $26 billion, as much as the nation had spent to fight World War I. Could there be any doubt—even among bulls, bargain hunters, optimists, and fools—that the Big Bull Market was indeed over, that the stock market crash was indeed a crash?

Political leaders paid close attention to the crash and its effects on the economy. In particular, President Hoover was concerned. A man of action, he began making moves that he hoped would limit the damage. His first effort was to lower income-tax rates by a full percentage point. For people in lower income brackets, this meant a cut of more than two-thirds in their tax bill. Hoover and his advisers hoped that if people spent less on taxes, they would have more money for investing and buying things again. However, taxes were so low at the time that the cut gave these ordinary Americans little extra money.

Next, Hoover organized a series of meetings of different groups of national leaders at the White House throughout late November 1929. Industrialists, railroad executives, utility company heads, major construction company executives, union officials, and officers of farmers' organizations came to Washington and met with the president. At these sessions, Hoover urged the executives to keep paying their employees the same wages and upgrading their factories and equipment.

As the business leaders left their White House sessions, they told newspaper reporters that they planned to keep their workers' pay rates where they were, just as President Hoover had asked. They all expressed their opinions that the business climate was sound. The reporters dutifully reported these plans and opinions to the nation.

One industrialist emerged from his November 21 meeting with President Hoover determined to astonish everyone with his cooperation, confidence, and generosity. This industrialist announced that he not only would maintain wages for the men on his assembly lines but in fact would *raise* them, from $6 to $7 a day. He also pledged to spend $25 million to expand his business operations. This industrialist was Henry Ford, founder and chairman of the Ford Motor Company. While Ford did set daily wages at $7 in his various automobile manufacturing plants, he did not raise the wages of workers who had already been making more than $7 a day. Instead, he found ways to move them to other departments and reduce their salaries.

Another captain of industry, John D. Rockefeller of Standard Oil,

The Bettmann Archive

A sign of the crash: 5,000 unemployed workers line up outside the State Labor Bureau Building in New York City looking for jobs.

had made no statement of any kind to the press for decades. Instead, he had left the management of the business to his son, John D. Rockefeller, Jr. In an attempt to restore public confidence just after the worst days of the crash, John, Sr., broke his usual silence to announce that he and his son were buying "sound common stocks."[1] Perhaps partly as a result, the Rockefeller family fortune shrank, over the next few years, to one-fifth its size before the crash.

The economy itself—the business climate—was weaker than business leaders like Rockefeller and government leaders like President Hoover suggested. The small percentage of Americans who had most of the country's money were the same people who had taken the biggest losses in the crash. The famous plunger Arthur Cutten, for instance, had lost $40 million in the crash. "King of the Bulls" William Durant had lost his entire fortune. Considering the losses that wealthy Americans had taken in the crash, it was hard to imagine where new investments in business could come from. When he heard about the Rockefellers, father and son, buying stock, comedian Eddie Cantor joked, "Sure, who else had any money left?"[2]

Another weak part of the economy was the banking system. There were many small independent banks in towns and cities all across the country. When bad times hit a region, these local banks were often forced out of business. If a drought in central Iowa ruined farmers' crops, they could not pay the mortgages on their lands and the loans on their tractors. The local bank that had made the loans went under. In the first six months of 1929, even before the crash, 346 local banks had failed. To make this problem worse, banks had made other kinds of loans—to the speculators who had bought stocks on margin. Many of these loans would never be paid off, now that so much of the value of the stock market had been lost.

In spite of the shaky economy, President Hoover announced on November 16, 1929: "Any lack of confidence in the economic future or the basic strength of business in the United States is foolish....Our national capacity for hard work and intelligent cooperation is ample guaranty of the future."[3] The chairman of an important Chicago bank said confidently, "This crash is not going to have much effect on business." The comedian Will Rogers said the crash wouldn't make much difference to ordinary folks, either: "Why, an old sow and litter of pigs make more people a living than all the steel and General Motors stock combined."[4] Economists, business people, and politicians all made optimistic remarks in public, but they did expect something of a slump, a period when fewer things would be made and sold.

Apart from the collapse of market values, little in the economy appeared to have changed between late October and mid-November. But as President Hoover had noticed, one thing that did change quickly was the national mood. Business people no longer felt certain that they could make money, and American shoppers no longer felt good about their incomes and their prospects. One financial magazine saw "a rather decided feeling of caution in the making of new commitments for the future."[5] The crash had hurt the nation's confidence.

Some of the damage was direct. The tone of the news changed after the crash. Instead of the stories they had carried a few months earlier of the people who had made a killing in the market, daily newspapers now featured the suicides of ruined speculators. The press was also full of stories of employees who had misused company funds to play the market and who were now being found out. In early November, the public read that James J. Riordan, an important financier and a friend of presidential candidate Al Smith, had been ruined by the crash—and had shot himself.

More important, the loss of confidence could—and did—have an indirect effect on the economy. Businesses suddenly found that raising money was much more difficult. A high percentage of well-off Americans, from the "King of the Bulls" to comedian Fanny Brice (the subject of the play and film *Funny Girl*), had lost heavily in the crash. As a result, they no longer had extra money to invest. Businesses had used some of

The Bettmann Archive

A familiar sight after the crash: Out-of-work men sell apples on the streets.

the money they had received from the sale of stocks during the boom to build new factories, hire new employees, and install new machinery. Now, both plungers like Arthur Cutten and small shareholders like Maggie Brennan were staying away from the brokerage office. The few people who were buying stocks were paying less for them. Businesses were

The Bettmann Archive

Ruined by the crash, unemployed workers demonstrate in front of the executive mansion in Albany, New York.

making smaller profits or losing money. Without profits, growth was impossible for businesses.

People who had lost large amounts of money stopped investing— and stopped spending as well. Wealthy people who had lost big in the crash had in many cases been on a buying spree earlier in the 1920s. Now that they were no longer buying, sales of gadgets and luxuries suffered. Sales of radios in New York City fell by half in the six remaining weeks of 1929 following the November 13 crash.

The loss of confidence also affected spending among less wealthy people, both in 1929 and later. During the boom years, installment-plan buying had become popular precisely because Americans had faith in the future. After the crash, when economic news began to seem frightening rather than hopeful, working Americans saved their money so they would have something to live on if they lost their jobs. They bought fewer things that they did not absolutely need. In North Carolina, Nannie Vaughn Turner stopped buying new fabric and started making her daughters' dresses out of the sacks that animal feed came in. Jane Yoder, growing up in a mining town in central Illinois with her father out of work, paid a lot of attention to shoes: "In rainy weather you just ran for it, you ran between the rain-drops or whatever. . . . You simply wore your old shoes if it was raining. Save the others. You always polished them and put shoe trees in them. . . . When the shoes are worn out, they're used around the house, and of the high heels, you cut the heels down and they're more comfortable."[6]

During the first three months of 1930, right after the crash, sales of all kinds were down 15 to 20 percent from the year before. If people were not buying the fabrics and shoes already in the stores, making more fab-rics and shoes was not profitable for businesses. These businesses then had to let some of their employees go. As people lost their jobs, their friends, relatives, and neighbors became even more fearful that they would be next—and they became even less likely to buy new shoes, cars, houses, or any of the other products of the nation's economy.

One example of what was happening in the days following the crash caught the attention of New York Governor Franklin Delano Roosevelt. His family estate was in a town called Hyde Park. A Hyde Park knitting mill turned out good-quality sweaters that sold for $9 or $10. Before the crash, the mill's 150 employees made a living and enjoyed steady work. The owner sold the sweaters in lots of 12 or 20 at a time to wholesalers in New York City, who in turn sold them to stores. After the crash, New Yorkers—like other Americans—stopped buying as many new clothes. The wholesalers cut back their orders to one or two sweaters at a time. The owner had to shut down between big orders. Eventually he had to lay off half his employees. He finally managed to get a contract to make 5,000 sweaters, at $2 apiece. The workers, who had made $20 or $25 a week before, now got only $5, and the owner made no profit at all. When Roosevelt visited the mill, he realized "how desperate people can become"[7] when they lost confidence and purchasing power.

From late November 1929 through February 1930, the stock market made something of a recovery. But the bad economic news continued to come in. In fact, the news kept getting worse. In March 1930, stock prices again took a nosedive. This time the people who were hurt were seasoned Wall Street professionals who had decided that owning stock was safe again. They had been mistaken.

Business leaders kept their promise to President Hoover and maintained wages at their current level—at least for a while. Workers lucky enough not to be laid off still had the same amount of money coming in. However, by the fall of 1931, most businesses had broken the no-wage-reduction pledge and began to lower employees' pay rates. Henry Ford, who had gotten so much publicity when he raised wages in 1929, cut back the total number of workers he employed in the 1930–1931 business year by 45,000—nearly 70 percent of the company's workers. And he made no public announcement when he cut the pay rates at his auto plants in October 1931. The effects of the stock market crash were beginning to be felt by both the bigtime industrialists and the ordinary working person. Could the optimism exhibited by the nation's leaders any longer be considered sincere or believable?

Chapter 6

The Great Depression

R obin Langston knew the Depression had really hit when the electricity went off. "My parents could no longer pay the $1 electric bill," he remembers.[1] The lights went out for many Americans in the years after the 1929 disaster—and in more ways than having their electricity turned off. In downtown New York City, a young girl walking with her father one January night in 1931 saw men, women, and children sleeping on newspapers outside an office building. "Why are they doing that, Daddy?" she asked. He didn't answer. When she looked up at him, she saw that he was crying.[2]

Arkansas farmer Clyde T. Ellis said, "The most valuable thing we lost was hope. A man can endure a lot if he still has hope....We had relatives who just gave up. Broke up homes, scattered to different states."[3]

People who had been wealthy before the crash also saw a difference in their lives. A southern woman who was a college student at the time remembers coming home at Christmas to find the family's telephone disconnected. By the following summer, her parents had laid off the cook and the cleaning woman.[4]

President Herbert Hoover gave the 1929 slump the name "depression." Before 1929, people had called a bad plunge of stock prices a "panic" or "crisis." Hoover thought "depression" sounded less threatening. He did

The Bettmann Archive

Evicted from their homes, thousands of families ruined by the crash ended up in makeshift camps.

The Bettmann Archive

The "Depression," meant to name a temporary decline in the economy, came to mean widespread despair, as lines of men looking for work became common.

not realize that he was changing the meaning of the term. Afterward "depression" came to mean a particularly severe and prolonged bad time for people and the economy. The term acquired additional significance when, in capitalized form, it was applied to a whole era.

Herbert Hoover continued as president through the first three years of the Depression. He and the other Republican leaders were unwilling to spend the federal government's money on relief for out-of-work or hungry people. They believed that it would be bad for the national economy to spend too much money and go into debt. The main thing the country needed to end the Depression, they thought, was a return of confidence.

Somehow the nation's leader could not inspire its people. Hoover's smile struck people as forced. He looked sober and cheerless. When he said, "I am convinced we have passed the worst and with continued effort we shall rapidly recover,"[5] he looked as though he did not believe this upbeat message. His fellow Americans did not believe it either.

Meanwhile, the economy's problems had spread from the factories and farms to the banks. Bank closings were increasing. In 1930 alone, 1,345 banks throughout the nation ran out of money and shut their doors, wiping out the savings of hundreds of thousands of people. The most important bank that failed, the Bank of the United States, held $1.5 million in New York City government deposits and $1 million in New York State money, as well as the life savings of half a million small investors. Before the bank was closed, there were runs at all its 57 branches, with long lines of panicked depositors trying to get at least some of their money out. This represented the largest bank failure in U.S. history to date. In 1931 bank failures rose to more than 2,000, with more than $1.5 billion in deposits.

By 1932, few people in the country remained untouched by the Depression. Everyone except the luckiest and most diehard speculators could see that the country needed new rules to control its economy. Financial institutions in general, and Wall Street in particular, had to work better. Even so, almost four years went by after the crash before

Congress passed the new laws the country needed so badly.

Everywhere, individual Americans were in need of the basics: food, clothing, and shelter. Herman Shumlin remembers a familiar sight in New York in those years: "Two or three blocks along Times Square, you'd see these men, silent, shuffling along in line. Getting this handout of coffee and doughnuts, dealt out from great trucks….Shabby clothes, but you could see they had been pretty good clothes."[6] Not only were people hungry, they were losing their apartments because they could not pay the rent. "There were so many evictions on the East Side," according to charity worker Dorothy Day, "that you couldn't walk down the streets without seeing furniture on the sidewalk."[7]

In the agricultural regions of the Midwest, farmers who could not keep up their mortgage payments saw their farms sold off. Sometimes their friends would help them beat the system. "They was having ten cent sales" in his part of Iowa in 1932, Harry Terrell recalled. "They'd put up a farmer's property and have a sale and all the neighbors'd come in, and they got the idea of spending twenty-five cents for a horse. They was paying ten cents for a plow. And when it was all over, they'd all give it back to him."[8]

Hungry and jobless people rioted in Oklahoma City and in the small town of England, Arkansas. In Pittsburgh, 2,500 people stood in line for food every day, and thousands more had to be turned away. Congress passed a bill authorizing drought relief for farm areas. By March 1931 the Red Cross, operating on charitable contributions from individuals, and the federal government combined were giving more than two million Americans—in both rural and urban America—drought relief. This was the federal government's first venture into providing relief, which had traditionally been made available only by state and local governments.

In 1932, the Democrats nominated New York Governor Franklin Delano Roosevelt as their candidate for president. In his acceptance speech, he said, "Our Republican leaders tell us economic laws cause panics which

The Bettmann Archive

A breadline in New York City reflects the hard conditions brought about by the crash.

no one can prevent. But while they prate of economic laws, men and women are starving."[9] He went on to promise a new deal for the American people.

During the campaign, Roosevelt never spelled out just what kind of changes this new deal would involve. Some people feared that he would

The Bettmann Archive

With no money for food, many people during the Depression had to rely on soup kitchens such as this one.

act to make the government take over the country's banking system. Others believed he could bring back prosperity overnight. Still others had little interest in what Roosevelt might or might not do. They simply believed that anyone would be better than Hoover, whom they blamed for the Depression.

Roosevelt easily defeated Hoover in an election that also sent a majority of Democrats to both houses of Congress. With Democrats in control of the legislature and the White House, the way was open for dramatic changes in policy and law.

A different approach was certainly needed. When Roosevelt took office in early 1933, state and city relief rolls totaled six million. Public welfare was more than twice what it had been in the 1920s. Yet it was not nearly enough. Since 1929, the country's total income, the worth of all goods and services being sold, had been cut in half. Unemployment was climbing. At the lowest point of the Depression, in early 1933, fully 25 percent of American workers were jobless.

The New York Stock Exchange was a prime candidate for reform. During the Big Bull Market, many companies selling stocks had made outrageous claims about their prospects. Others released little hard information about the securities they traded on the Exchange. No law had protected investors from this kind of fraud. The members of pools had also been acting dishonestly when they made themselves rich by fooling the public into buying stock at inflated prices. All that changed during Franklin Roosevelt's presidency, after Congress passed the Securities Act of 1933 and the Securities Exchange Act of 1934.

These laws required companies to make public many dealings that had been kept secret, banned pools entirely, and gave the Federal Reserve Board power to set margin requirements. The Fed now decided what percentage of a stock's price investors would have to put up in cash. The Securities Acts also created a new government agency, the Securities and Exchange Commission (SEC), to regulate stock trading. The SEC became the policeman on the Wall Street beat. It made sure that the sellers of securities behaved themselves. Newspapers summed up the effect in the words "Let the seller beware,"[10] a new twist on the older notion "Let the buyer beware."

One of the new agency's jobs was to make sure that stock-issuing companies gave out accurate information about the securities they offered for sale. The SEC prevented companies from making wildly optimistic claims about how much money they would earn in the future. Investors who felt that companies had deceived them could take the companies to court. If they could prove that they had been cheated, the court could award them money—and the company would have to pay. Of course, the SEC did not entirely prevent unwise investments from being offered, or investors with poor judgment from buying them. But the new agency tried to protect investors from outright fraud.

Other important reforms came in banking. Many banks ran out of money after the crash because they had divisions that bought and sold securities. These banks had been investing depositors' money in stocks, with disastrous results. A new law, the Glass-Steagall Act of 1933, made it illegal for banks to buy and sell securities. Banks that dealt in investments became separate from the commercial banks that most Americans depended on for their day-to-day financial security.

The same law gave the federal government the power to insure bank deposits. A new government insurance company, the Federal Deposit Insurance Corporation, protected deposits in the nation's banks up to a certain amount. If a bank went out of business, the government made sure that depositors got their money back promptly.

The Roosevelt administration made other important changes in the way the country worked. Many of these changes gave new means of protection to ordinary Americans who face unexpected problems, such as losing their jobs or becoming disabled. The Social Security system, unemployment compensation, workmen's compensation, and agricultural

The Bettmann Archive

A refugee family travels around the country in their truck looking for temporary work and a place to live.

subsidies all date from this period. Other New Deal programs put millions of unemployed people to work on government projects.

The overall effect was that, for the first time, Americans saw their government as partly responsible for the welfare of all the nation's people. In 1931, before Roosevelt became president, he had said, "I assert that modern society, acting through its Government, owes the definite obligation to prevent the starvation or the dire want of any of its fellow men and women who try to maintain themselves but cannot."[11]

No single reform, in and of itself, could bring an end to the Depression. After 1933 the economy improved, but only in small degrees. Not until 1942, after the United States had entered World War II, did employment and production really recover to the levels before the crash. What President Hoover had naively labeled a depression became not just the Depression, but the Great Depression.

Chapter 7

Can It Happen Again?

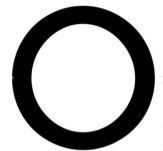n October 20, 1987, 58 years after the crash of 1929, those older citizens who remembered that disaster may have had a sense of long-delayed replay. The headline of the *New York Times* that day read: STOCKS PLUNGE 508 POINTS, A DROP OF 22.6%; 604 MILLION VOLUME NEARLY DOUBLES RECORD.

Newspapers were quick to point out similarities to the 1929 crash. During the 1980s, a Republican administration had once again cut income tax rates on the rich, and the rich had invested their windfall not in businesses but in the purchase of common stock. Once again, this had created a long, strong bull market. Once again, prices had been on an irregular downward track since the end of the summer. And once again, the "ticker"—or, rather, the instrument that had replaced it, the computer system of the New York Stock Exchange—fell behind the action on the floor. The panic of not having up-to-the-minute prices for particular stocks helped push prices farther down, just as it had in 1929.

There were other similarities. Stock prices had bounced back briefly after Black Thursday, 1929, and they did so again in 1987. The Dow-Jones industrial average regained 63 percent of its loss in the next two business days in 1929, while in 1987, the average gained back 57 percent of the lost ground in the same period. There was even a "classic" suicide in 1987, as one broker who had lost badly in the crash jumped from his office window.

The aftermath was different this time around, though. In 1929 prices plunged for two weeks and took another dive six months later. This did not happen in 1987. Instead, once stock prices had rebounded, they remained near the new level for some months and then began to climb again. Nor did the nation's economy sink into another Great Depression, even though the initial drop in the market had been as bad as the one in 1929. Why were things different this time?

For one thing, many of the investors in the 1987 stock market were buying and selling very large amounts of stock. More than half the people trading stocks in the market then were dealing in blocks of 10,000 shares or more. People with so much stock to trade were usually professional traders managing other people's stocks for them. They invested money for insurance companies, pension funds, or mutual funds—group investments similar to the investment trust of the 1920s but less shaky.

These traders were different from the small investors and the players of the 1920s. Before the 1929 crash, individual speculators themselves decided what they would have their brokers buy and sell for them. In 1987 the responsibility for making decisions about many large investments was in the hands of professional managers, not individual speculators. As experienced professionals investing other people's money, these managers were less likely to panic. They continued investing even when stock prices went down, attempting to move the money they had charge of into more profitable securities. This made the market less shaky than it was in 1929 and may have contributed to the faster recovery.

Also, the Great Depression was so severe and so painful that it taught the country a lesson it had not forgotten, even 58 years later. The reforms of the Stock Exchange and the banking system that were made in the 1930s remained in place. In fact, the new laws had been improved and expanded since then. The Federal Reserve Board had the power in 1987 to control the requirements for the percentage of a stock's purchase price that an investor had to pay in cash. In the 1920s this margin was sometimes as low as 10 percent. By contrast, an investor who wanted to buy stock on margin in 1987 was required to put up at least 50 percent of the price in cash.

Economists John Kenneth Galbraith[1] and Moses Abramowitz,[2] among others, pointed out another legacy of the 1930s that helped prevent disaster in 1987. In the many decades since Roosevelt's presidency, under Democratic and Republican administrations alike, the legacy of the Roosevelt New Deal, known as the "safety net," had remained in place. Programs such as Social Security, Medicare, unemployment compensation, and Aid to Families with Dependent Children protected people from the worst effects of poverty. They also represented an important way of receiving income not directly connected to the ups and downs of the business world.

People receiving Social Security checks in 1987, for instance, felt confident that they would have at least some money to spend whether or not the 1987 crash sent the country's economy into a depression. With money in their pockets, they were more upbeat about the future than many Americans were in the Depression years.

Will there be another stock market crash? John Kenneth Galbraith[3] and Gordon Axon[4] are among those who say probably. Once the memory of the 1987 plunge fades in investors' memories, people will become more optimistic and take more risks with their money. This in turn can lead to greed and inflated stock prices—prices higher than they should be for a company's worth.

People's feelings continue to influence their decisions about trading stock. As long as there seems to be a way to make big money in the market, there will also be the risk that some investors will get carried away. James Sterngold wrote in 1987, "Human emotion, a force undeterred by legislation or regulation, still drives the stock market." Investors, he said, are unpredictable and always will be.[5]

Some experts think it is unlikely that an economic disaster on the scale of the Great Depression will follow a future stock market crash, any more than a depression followed the crash of 1987. Shortly after that event, William LeFevre wrote in the *New York Times* that our society had changed a lot as a result of the Great Crash and the Great Depression. Elected officials had made new laws partly to prevent anything quite as bad from ever happening again.[6] LeFevre said that these changes kept the crash in 1987 from being as big a disaster as the one in 1929. Ohers who have written about the crash and the Depression, such as William Klingaman, take the opposite view: that many soothing words about how such an economic disaster could never happen were spoken before—in 1929.[7]

The philosopher George Santayana said, "Those who do not remember the past are condemned to repeat it." Up to the present, the changes our society made after the Great Crash have protected us from a repeat performance. But historians and experts can only tell us about the past. They cannot confidently predict the future.

★ ★ ★

SOURCE NOTES

Chapter 1

1. William K. Klingaman, *1929: The Year of the Great Crash* (New York: Harper & Row, 1989), p. 131.
2. From the *Saturday Evening Post* and quoted in Ethan Mordden, *That Jazz!* (New York: Putnam, 1978), pp. 70–71.

Chapter 2

1. John Kenneth Galbraith, *The Great Crash, 1929* (Boston: Houghton Mifflin, 1972), p. 12.
2. Personal anecdote.
3. Personal anecdote.

Chapter 3

1. Edward Robb Ellis, *A Nation in Torment: The Great American Depression, 1929–1939* (New York: Coward-McCann, 1970), p. 32.
2. Ibid., p. 30.
3. Klingaman, p. 54.
4. Ibid.
5. Ellis, p. 31.

Chapter 4

1. Ellis, p. 43.
2. Klingaman, p. 233.
3. Personal anecdote.
4. Ellis, p. 70.
5. Robert S. McElvaine, *The Great Depression: America, 1929–1941* (New York: Times Books, 1983), p. 46.
6. Ellis, p. 71.
7. Ibid., p. 72.
8. Ibid., p. 78.
9. Galbraith, p. 111.
10. Ibid., p. 112.
11. Ellis, p. 88.
12. Klingaman, p. 269.

Chapter 5

1. Galbraith, p. 124.
2. Klingaman, p. 291.
3. Ibid., pp. 300–301.
4. Ellis, p. 81.
5. Klingaman, p. 298.
6. Studs Terkel, *Hard Times, An Oral History of the Great Depression* (New York: Pantheon, 1986), p. 86.
7. Ellis, p. 123.

Chapter 6

1. Terkel, p. 89.
2. Gene Smith, *The Shattered Dream: Herbert Hoover and the Great Depression* (New York: Morrow, 1970), p. 80.
3. Terkel, p. 230.
4. Ibid., p. 153.
5. Smith, p. 59.
6. Terkel, p. 381.
7. Ibid., p. 303.
8. Ibid., p. 214.
9. Smith, p. 122.
10. McElvaine, p. 163.
11. Ellis, p. 539.

Chapter 7

1. "Stocks Plunge 508 Points, a Drop of 22.6%; 604 Million Volume Nearly Doubles Record," the *New York Times,* October 10, 1987, p. 1.
2. Moses Abramowitz, "No Panic Now," the *New York Times,* November 1, 1987, p. 21.
3. Galbraith, p. 194.
4. Gordon V. Axon, *The Stock Market Crash of 1929* (New York: Mason and Lipscomb, 1974), p. 134.
5. James Sterngold, "Stock Plunge Leads to Look at the Safety Net," the *New York Times,* December 14, 1987, p. 1.
6. William LeFevre, "Seeking Clues to the Market's Future," the *New York Times,* December 27, 1987, p. C-10.
7. Klingaman, p. xvi.

FOR FURTHER READING

Axon, Gordon V. *The Stock Market Crash of 1929.* New York: Mason and Lipscomb, 1974.

Ellis, Edward Robb. *A Nation in Torment: The Great American Depression, 1929–1939.* New York: Coward-McCann, 1970.

Galbraith, John Kenneth. *The Great Crash, 1929.* Boston: Houghton Mifflin, 1972.

Goodman, Paul. *America in the Twenties: The Beginnings of Contemporary America.* New York: Holt Reinhart and Winston, 1971.

Klingaman, William K. *1929: The Year of the Great Crash.* New York: Harper & Row, 1989.

Levien, J. R. *Anatomy of a Crash, 1929.* New York: Traders Press, 1966.

McElvaine, Robert S. *The Great Depression: America, 1929–1941.* New York: Times Books, 1983.

Mordden, Ethan. *That Jazz! An Idiosyncratic Social History of the American Twenties.* New York: Putnam, 1978.

Perrett, Geoffrey. *America in the Twenties: A History.* New York: Simon and Schuster, 1982.

Sloat, Warren. *1929, America Before the Crash.* New York: Macmillan, 1979.

Smith, Gene. *The Shattered Dream: Herbert Hoover and the Great Depression.* New York: Morrow, 1970.

Terkel, Studs. *Hard Times: An Oral History of the Great Depression.* New York: Pantheon Books, 1986.

INDEX

DISCARDED

PEACHTREE

J 973.916 MILLICHAP PTREE
Millichap, Nancy
The stock market crash of
1929

AUG 07 1995

Atlanta-Fulton Public Library